D1242198

William Collins Sons & Co Ltd
London · Glasgow · Sydney · Auckland
Toronto · Johannesburg

For Katie with love

Also compiled by Nanette Newman

GOD BLESS LOVE
LOTS OF LOVE
VOTE FOR LOVE
ALL OUR LOVE

The front cover drawing
is by Suzanne aged 10.

Endpaper design
by Sarah and Emma Forbes

First published 1980
© Bryan Forbes Limited 1980
ISBN 0 00 195292 7

Printed in Hong Kong by
South China Printing Co.

Foreword

I hope the reader will enjoy this, my fifth
collection in the series, which throws some more
confusion on the age old mystery that began - so
we are told - with Adam and Eve and is still
more popular, thank goodness, than wars, hate
and politics.

I am grateful to all the young contributors
for giving me the Facts of Love as they
see them.

Nanette Newman

The Facts of Love

A collection of children's sayings
compiled by

NANETTE NEWMAN

COLLINS St James's Place, London

I shall see how I like being marrid
and if I dont like it I will try
sumthing else.

Mark aged 11

My sister only wants to get
married beause she's a
rotten show off.

Peter aged 9

To have a baby you have to make love to someone who doesn't mind

Marianne aged 9

first of all you get in love get married
and get a baby or you can do it
the other way round.

Peter aged 9

some people have babies just
buecause their friends say they
shud

Naomi aged 8

If you dount want babies you
should practice contradiction

Lynne aged 9

it is eggier to have a baby

if you a cat

Tricie aged 6

To have a baby the Mother has to lay an egg then the mail cracks it.

Alison aged 8

when you're pregnant you become sicker and faxter and nastier every day

Marianne aged 9

I nearly know how to have babies but we don't do it till next term

Frances aged 7

you can't talk about babies being made until you are in the 4th form.

Davina aged 10

don't know how a baby gets there and I think Id rather be serprized.

Claire aged 8

if You put a Man and a Woman in bed together one of them will have a baby

Paul aged 6

The man next door has a baby in his tummy but it never comes out

Janet aged 6

If you want to have a baby goto the library

Pierre aged 8

You mustn't giv Yoew born bady
Sweets its a waste.

Lisa aged 4

Some babies dont Want to be born but there
is nothing they can do ab.out it

David aged 6

Some babys come out
in nighties and boots

Juliet aged 4

MY sister came out too early
So she lived in a glass
house for 3 Weeks

Jake aged 5

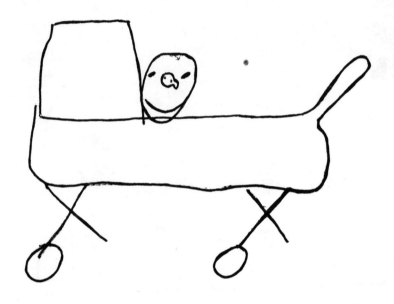

MY brother looked horrible
when was born but I didn't say so
because they wouldn't let me
change him.

Leigh aged 6

A baby comes out of the
mummy tummy and bites the Doctor,
and the Docor smacks it.

Edward aged 6

You should n't have
babies on Sunday because
God wants you to rest.

Merino aged 7

Babies come out of your tummy
on a piece of string.

Graham aged 7

Joseeph's wife Mary had an
immaculate contraption

Cathy aged 7

Jesus was born witha yellow
frill round his head like
his Mother

Jeffrey aged 5

mary had Jesus so that she
could get a house.

Christine aged 6

The 3 kings gave Jesus
nasty Christmas presents

Loise aged 6

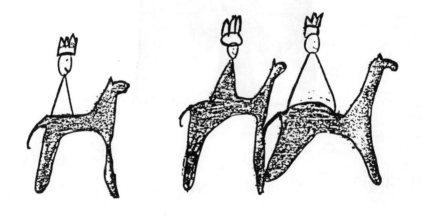

people   like   to have
babies   for   christmas

Anne aged 4

If you don't love your baby it won't come and visit you when your old

Noura aged 7

My brother was born even though I didnt want him.

Noel aged 6

I want to swop my sister for something better.

Alex aged 4

mothers and other nasty people frighten children to make them be good

Ben aged 6

You Should never hit a baby
because it can't hit back

Mike aged 6

I think the Pope must have been a good baby.

Elizabeth aged 6

My Granny cries when she's
happy and when she's sad
she just stares.

Davina aged 10

My Grann is in love with
the pope but he's never goin to marry

Richard aged 6

I dont think you know you hav
been happy until youre not

Mark aged 11

I dont know if I am happy or not
so I suppos I am

Joanne aged 10

"Some people never

laugh with their faces

Lynne aged 9

People go on too much about being happy

so every body wants to be it all the time

ans they cant So they get Sad

Adrian aged 8

My Mummys friend took a Husband away and never braugt Him bak

Shelley aged 6

My Mummy and Daddy dont I ove each other they only love me

Layla aged 8

I am helping my Mummy choose m next Daddy.

Anna aged 5

2 peepul
follin in
love
xx
x

people usually Want to die
because they like being buried

Claire aged 8

It would be nice if when you died
you blew away like a leaf so
People wouldn't have to clean
up after you.

Nigel aged 8

Jesus wanted people to be happy but
he didnt tell them how to do it

Naomi aged 8

when my sister was born she
decided to go straight back to heaven.

Lucinda aged 5